Fini Saves The Lambs

Hanelie Weir

Published by 80% Weird Books.

Words and illustration by Hanelie Weir.

To my brother Riaan, who still lives on this
Karoo farm and cares for the environment
and the animals with a huge father heart.

How to read this book:

enjoy the full story and illustrations through the middle section of this book

or

if you are pressed for time or a new reader, only read the shortened blocked version at the top

or

allow the scripture portions at the bottom to highlight some exciting Biblical truths.

Fini the meerkat lives in a hole under the ground. He wakes up early every morning and pops out the hole – ready for the new day.

Fini lives in a cosy burrow on a large sheep farm in the Karoo. He shares his underground home with his dad and mum, a few brothers and sisters, his grandparents, his uncles, aunts, cousins and other distant meerkat relatives.

The early mornings are quite noisy and busy and Fini is glad to escape up one of the exits to see what the new day will bring.

"Before you created the world and the mountains were made, from the beginning to the end you are God." (Psalm 90:2 NIrV Kids' Quest)

One morning, Fini heard from his friend Erlank the tortoise that there was trouble.

Early one morning, Fini found his friend Erlank staring into the sky. Fini looked up just in time to see the majestic Black Eagle taking off. He became smaller and smaller, and disappeared over the mountain.

Erlank said in his deep, slow voice, "Oh Fini, important news. There is trouble in the Narra camp."

"You won't have to be afraid ... The Lord is the one who keeps you safe. So, let the Most
NIrV Kids' Quest)

Erlank said that the lamb could be in danger.

The sparrows brought the news to Black Eagle. Fini knew this was serious, because the Narra camp is where the new-born lambs are kept – the last camp before the dreaded mountain.

High God be like a home to you. Then no harm will come to you." (Psalm 91:5,9 and 10

Fini wanted to investigate, so he thought of a plan.

"We must investigate straight away!" Fini said.

Erlank thought and thought, but before he could say anything, Fini had scampered off through the riverbed and was halfway up the bank on the other side. This was his favourite thinking spot. He could see the Narra camp and the mountain in the distance, and sitting up on his hind legs, he could even see his home. By the time Erlank had finally caught up with him, Fini had thought of a plan.

"Are you tired? Worn out? Burned out on religion? Come to me. Get away with me and you'll recover your life. I'll show you how to take a real rest. Walk with me and work with me – watch how I do it. Learn the unforced rhythms of grace. I won't lay anything heavy or ill-fitting on you. Keep company with me and you'll learn to live freely and lightly." (Matthew 11:28 The Message (MSG))

They needed all their friends to help. First, they wanted to ask Miki the rock monitor, but he was not at his usual place by the waterhole.

They needed to gather all their friends to help. A real team effort, Erlank called it. Fini ran off to find Miki the rock monitor, but he was nowhere to be found.

Down at the shallow waterhole, where Miki usually cools off, there were only footprints in the mud. Fini sped off toward the thorn tree thicket, hoping to find Kingsley the young kudu.

When Fini found Kingsley the kudu, he was too scared to come out of his hiding place among the thorn trees.

Kingsley never left the safety of the trees and no matter how hard Fini tried to get him to come along, Kingsley refused.

He whispered to Fini, "I am just a kudu, and I understand that the lambs could be in danger, but I just don't think I can make a difference – you don't need me."

With that, Kingsley turned to move a bit further into the bush.

"God did not give us a spirit that makes us weak and fearful. He gave us a spirit that gives us power and love. It helps us control ourselves." (2 Timothy 1:7 NIrV Kids' Quest)

Just when Fini wanted to give up, he saw Black Eagle, and knew he had to carry on.

By now, Fini felt discouraged and thought that the problem was far too big for his little meerkat plan.

He was about to turn back, when a shadow caught his eye. He looked up toward the mountain and saw the majestic form of Black Eagle gliding through the sky.

For a moment, even the brightness of the Karoo sun was blocked out. Fini's heart started beating faster, because he knew he was not alone.

“He who dwells in the shelter of the Most High will rest in the shadow of the Almighty.
International Version (NIV))

Up the animal trail Fini went, looking for Jana the springhare. She wants to help!

Now that Fini had seen Black Eagle, he made his way past the big windmill and down the lane where the spiky num-num bushes grow. He hoped to find Jana here. But Jana found him first. She jumped out from behind a Karoo bush. She gave him such a fright that he scurried into a nearby mouse hole. It was only when he heard the giggling of Jana behind him, that he backed out of the tiny hole.

When Jana heard about Fini's problem, she was keen to help. Jana was the happiest and most eager of the wild animals. "Such a big adventure needs lots of hands (and feet)," she said.

I will say of the Lord, 'He is my fortress, my God in whom I trust'." (Psalm 91:1-2 New

Jana wasn't sure how they would solve the problem.

On their way past the shearing shed, Jana suddenly commented: "Fini, you are a small animal… and I am quite small too. We're even smaller than a lamb. Fini, how are we going to solve the problem?"

Fini stared into the distance, where he saw the sheep grazing peacefully. "Jana, I don't know, but I'm sure by the time we get there, we will have a plan."

"Thank you, Father, Lord of heaven and earth, you've concealed your ways from sophisticates unskilled)" (Matthew 11:25 The Message(MSG), AMPC)

and know-it-alls, but spelled them out clearly to ordinary people (to the childish, untaught and

"Don't love the world's ways. Don't love the world's goods. Love of the wanting your own way, wanting everything for yourself, wanting to set for eternity." (1 John 2 The Message (MSG))

While Fini and Jana rested, they saw Miki the rock monitor having a swim on the wrong side of the fence.

The two friends decided to rest at a good lookout spot. Fini sat up on his hind legs and saw the fence in the distance. He saw something else, too – it was Miki. Fini could not believe his eyes. There Miki was on the wrong side of the fence, looking fresh and clean.

Jana said, "He probably went for a swim in the fountain. You know how much he loves water."

world squeezes out love for the Father. Practically everything that goes on in the world – appear important – has nothing to do with the Father ... but whoever does what God wants is

It was very dangerous and selfish of Miki to go up there. Miki quickly crawled through the fence and followed the trail back home.

"But Jana, surely Miki knows that it's dangerous to go into the mountain camp? That's where Tanala lives."

Miki quickly crawled through the fence and made his way down the small animal trail. He was surprised to find Fini and Jana so far from home, but he did not even stop to listen to them. He was in a hurry to get down to the riverbed for his afternoon sleep. Fini was not going to let Miki's selfishness get him down. So, the meerkat and springhare team carried on along the trail.

"Each day is God's gift. It's all you get in exchange for the hard work of staying alive. is your last and only chance at it." (Ecclesiastes 9:10 The Message (MSG))

Jana bounced like a little kangaroo right in amongst the sheep. She was always happy and full of fun.

Now, springhares don't just walk along like their meerkat friends. What they do best is to hop or take big leaps. So Fini let Jana bounce along ahead of him.

As he laughed at her bouncing tricks, she suddenly hopped straight toward the sheep. Fini stared in amazement and wondered if Jana knew that wild animals don't usually mix with farm animals. But Jana just bounced around in her merry way – right in between the flock of sheep. She playfully hopped up to the small lambs but was soon surrounded by the big sheep.

Make the most of each one! Whatever turns up, grab it and do it. And heartily! This

Fini reached the fence and discovered a big hole, so big that a dangerous jackal could fit through.

Fini was eager to get to the fence and left Jana to play. When he finally arrived, he saw the big hole in the tall wire fence. He also noticed all the animal tracks around it. Fini stared at the hole which was about twice his height and as wide as himself, Jana and Erlank together – just the right size for a cunning jackal like Tanala to fit through, he thought with a shudder.

He suddenly thought of his friend Erlank and wondered if he would ever get there.

"But those who trust in the Lord will receive new strength. They will run and not get tired.

They will walk and not grow weak." (Isaiah 40:31 NIrV Kids' Quest, Amplified)

Jana brought one of the sheep to help. He had big curly horns.

Fini found a heap of big rocks nearby and scrambled to the top to get a better view. He was about to pop up onto his hind legs when he heard a noise behind him. He turned around and saw Jana standing there with a big smile on her face. But what surprised him even more was the big ram that stood next to her. "Jana, what are you doing? You know we don't mix with farm animals – we don't even understand their language."

Jana just laughed and said, "Fini, with a pair of big curly horns like that and a body ten times as big as ours, he must be good for something."

"You're blessed when you can show people how to cooperate instead of compete or fight. That's when you discover who you really are, and your place in God's family." (Blessed are the peacemakers) (Matthew 5:9 The Message (MSG))

”Let us not become tired of doing good.
(Galatians 6:9 NIrV Kids’ Quest)

Erlank the tortoise finally arrived and gave Fini a clever plan.

As Fini and the old ram stared at each other, Fini heard a familiar voice in the distance. It was Erlank! "Hi there! So, you thought of a plan all on your own."

Fini wondered what he meant as he got down from the pile of rocks to welcome his friend.

"I see you were about to roll that big rock in front of the hole, Fini – what a clever plan."

Fini looked back to see the rock he was sitting on and then wondered why he hadn't thought of it – it really was a clever plan.

At the right time we will gather a crop if we don't give up."

Kingsley the kudu came with Erlank to help.

"But Erlank that rock is far too heavy for us to move and the sun is setting," Fini said, as the large shadow of night crept down the mountain.

"Oh, I don't think you should worry about that, Fini," Erlank said.

It was only then that Fini noticed the tall, nervous figure behind Erlank. It was Kingsley the young kudu bull. On his way past the thorn-tree thicket, Erlank had spent some time with Kingsley. Erlank's friendship and patience encouraged Kingsley to take a brave step and follow him.

"Father of orphans, champion of widows, is God in His Holy house. God makes homes for the homeless, leads prisoners to freedom." (Psalm 68:5-6 The Message (MSG))

All the friends helped to push a big rock in front of the hole. What a clever plan!

Kingsley was still a bit nervous and unsure, but when Fini and Erlank explained the plan, Kingsley was the first to step forward. The ram was a bit confused at first, but soon realised the plan. Erlank and Fini looked around and found the perfect rock and started putting everybody to work. Kingsley shoved with his strong horns on one side, the ram on the other side, and all the others pawed and pushed wherever they could reach.

Slowly the rock started moving, closer and closer to the fence until it covered the hole perfectly. And so it was that all the friends – big and small, wild and not so wild, helped fix the hole. It was indeed a big team effort.

"Get out the message – God Rules! He put the world on a firm foundation; He treats every tree of he forest in the choir. An extravaganza before God as he comes, as he (Psalm 96:10-13 The Message (MSG))

everyone fair and square ... Let wilderness turn cartwheels, animals, come dance, put comes to set everything right on earth, set everything right, treat everyone fair."

Finally, the lambs would be safe tonight – now Fini can go home to his own cozy bed.

As night-time shadows began to fold around them, the animals started making their way home. Fini and Erlank climbed onto the rock to inspect their hard work. "Look how peaceful the lambs are Fini," Erlank said.

Fini saw the sheep huddling up close for the night and he knew the lambs would be safe. Black Eagle swooped overhead once more, and Fini knew his job was done. Fini and Jana scurried back down the animal trail to get home and Fini suddenly wondered where Erlank would be sleeping for the night...

Can you match the footprints to the animals?

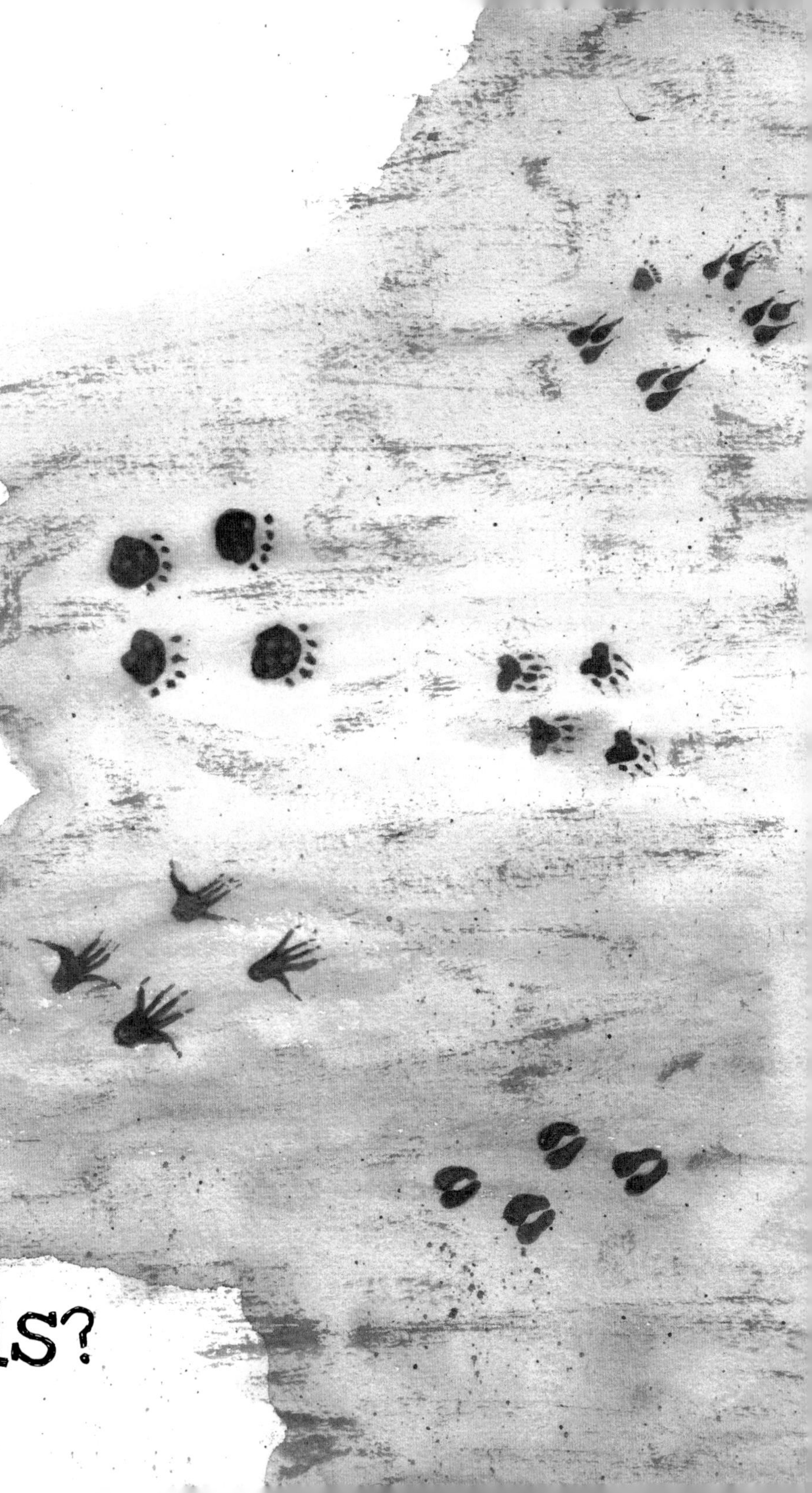

Questions to develop higher-order thinking skills

Did you know that a group of meerkat is called a mob?

Do you know the names of any other groups of animals?

Who do you think was **scared** in the story?

Who do you think was **brave**?

Who do you think was **wise**?

Who do you think was **selfish**?

Who **believed**?

Who was **happy**?

(lonely, sad, angry, calm)

Why do you think Fini did not give up?

What was the big trouble?

How did Fini get the other animals to help him?

What would you have done to protect the lambs?

Where do you think Erlank the tortoise would sleep?
(E.g. in a hole, under a bush, in a log, in his shell...)

About the author

Hanelie Weir is a Scottish South African living in Iceland. She grew up on a sheep farm in the beautiful South African Karoo area where plant and animal life adapted to survive in a very low rainfall area, and where people danced in the rain and played in muddy puddles when the rain did arrive.

She now works as an Early Learning Practitioner with a passion to help and support children who think and process differently.

If you've enjoyed this book, please help to spread the word and consider leaving a review on Amazon or any other suitable forum. These are a huge help to authors. You can keep up with Hanelie's news and share your thoughts on Fini's story on her author Facebook page.

“This book was written more than seventeen years ago, but I had no illustrator to take the idea to publishing. When my husband was offered a job opportunity in Iceland, my school agreed to give me a two-year career break to support him. I’ve used this time to learn watercolour in order to do the illustrations myself. It has been a hugely rewarding learning curve as I can page through this book and recognise how my paintings have progressed through the year.”

Made in the USA
Middletown, DE
13 November 2025

21381431R00022